WRITING works!

Open-ended classroom activities

Linda Polon

LONGMAN

Dedication

My Mom, Edie Wolff, who always encourages me to write, write, and do more writing

Lissette, a writer fan of mine

Aileen Cantwell, my favorite co-author

Gail Hendricks, a wonderful friend

Laura Strom—my editor, who is always on the other end of the line when I need advice

Addison Wesley Longman Australia Pty Limited
95 Coventry Street
South Melbourne 3205 Australia

Offices in Sydney, Brisbane and Perth, and associated companies throughout the world.

Copyright © Addison Wesley Longman Australia Pty Limited 1998
First published 1998

Originally published by Good Year Books 1998, 1900 East Lake Avenue, Glenview, IL 60025

All rights reserved. Except under the conditions described in the Copyright Act 1968 of Australia and subsequent amendments, no part of this publication may be reproduced, stored in a retrieval system or transmitted in any form or by any means, electronic, mechanical, photocopying, recording or otherwise, without the prior permission of the copyright owner. Permission is hereby granted to the purchaser to reproduce each blackline master from the book in quantities suitable for non-commercial classroom use.

Designed by Street Level Studio
Illustrated by Street Level Studio and Daniella Bauman
Cover design by Daniella Bauman
Set in ITC Benguiat Gothic
Produced by Addison Wesley Longman Australia Pty Limited
Printed in Malaysia

ISBN: 0 7339 0374 6

Every effort has been made to trace and acknowledge copyright. However, should any infringement have occurred, the publishers tender their apologies and invite copyright owners to contact them.

The publisher's policy is to use **paper manufactured from sustainable forests**

Table of Contents

How to Use This Book 5
Mini-lessons and Story Starters
Writing a Sentence 6
   Declarative
   Interrogative
   Imperative
   Exclamatory
   Sentence Review
   Simple Subject
   Predicate
   Subject/Predicate Review
Nouns 15
   Common and Proper
   Plural Nouns
   Irregular Plural Nouns
   Possessive Nouns—Singular and Plural
Abbreviations 21
Verbs 22
   Linking Verbs
   Tenses—Present, Past, Future
   Agreement
   Plural Endings
   Auxiliary Verbs
   Irregular Past Tense
Synonyms and Antonyms 31
Contractions 33
Pronouns 34
Adjectives 38
   Adjectives
   Irregular Adjectives
Homophones and Homographs 43
Adverbs 45
   Adverbs
   Adverbs v. Adjectives
   Adverb and Adjective Review
Compound Words 50
Double Negatives 51
Prefixes 52
Suffixes 53

Table of Contents continued

Prepositions 54
Conjunctions 55
Interjections 56
Run-on Sentences 57
Compound Subjects 58
Compound Predicates 60
Commas 63
Onomatopoeia 64
Similes 65
Metaphors 66
Personification 67
Alliteration 68
Review of Skills from pp. 62–67 70
Paragraphs 71
Writing Autobiography 73
Writing Personal Narrative 74
Writing Short Story 75
Writing Biographical Sketch 78
Writing Tall Tales 79
Writing Fables 81
Writing Character Sketches 82
Writing Plots 84
Writing Reports 86
   Book Report
   Research Report
Writing Instructions 88
Writing Different Kinds of Letters 89
   Friendly Letter
   Business Letter
   Thank-You Note
   Invitation
Filling Out Forms 93
Writing Dialogue 94
Writing a Play 95
List of More Open-ended Story Starters 96

How to Use This Book

The purpose of this book is to help students improve their writing and grammar skills while enjoying the writing process. Included in each writing activity is a grammar mini-lesson to help students improve their grammar skills and use of the language. Students are encouraged to write using their newly acquired or reinforced language skills to help their stories come alive.

This book is arranged sequentially and, except for one or two pages, should be used in order. After students have written, they should review it, looking to see if they have incorporated what was taught in the mini-lesson. If they find applications of the skill, they should underline them in their writing as directed. If they do not find that application, then they should revise or rewrite to incorporate examples of the skill. This not only teaches the students the importance of rereading their writing, but also gives them practice in revision and rewriting. Incorporating the skills taught in the mini-lessons will give students an appreciation for the variety of structures and components of sentences. This will lead to more effective use of the language when they write.

On the last page of the book, there is a list of open ended story starters to use either for free writing exercises or to reinforce concepts that need extra attention. As a free writing exercise, you may simply write the story starter on a blackboard and let the students take it from there. Or to reinforce a concept, have the students review their completed story and revise, reusing any of the mini-lessons that they need extra help on.

If there is not enough room for students to do their work on the worksheets, they can continue their work on another piece of paper.

Declarative

Name _____ **Date** _____

> A sentence that expresses a complete thought, begins with a capital letter and ends with a full stop is called a declarative sentence. ("**T**he lemonade fizzed in my face. **I** enjoyed walking in the warm ocean.) An incomplete sentence does not tell anything. (in the corner of the room/a friend yelled at)

Write a story using one of the story ideas below. Title your story and draw a picture to illustrate it. Afterward, review your story and see if you can find any declarative sentences. If so, underline them. If not, try revising or rewriting to incorporate some.

- If you owned a store, what kind would it be?
- What if you lived during the dinosaur period?
- You have invented something that will help people. What is it and what does it do?

Title: _____

_____

_____

_____

_____

_____

_____

_____

_____

_____

_____

_____

6

Writing a Sentence

Name _____ Date _____

> A declarative sentence expresses a complete thought, begins with a capital letter and ends with a full stop. (**I** always use the scooper when I walk the dog.)

Write a story using one of the story ideas below. Title your story and draw a picture to illustrate it. Afterward, review your story and see if you can find any declarative sentences. If so, underline them. If not, try revising or rewriting to incorporate some.

- If I could be famous in any sport. . .
- If I was an inanimate object (something not alive). . .
- If I was on TV, I would do and feel. . .

Title: _____

_____

_____

_____

_____

_____

_____

_____

_____

_____

_____

_____

_____

Writing a Sentence

7

Interrogative

Name _____ **Date** _____

> An interrogative, or asking, sentence is a sentence that asks a question. It begins with a capital letter and ends with a question mark. (**W**here did you go**?**) Most asking sentences begin with the words: *how, why, are, is, which, where, when, have, did, could, would, should, wouldn't, couldn't, what, will, does, didn't* or *do*.

Write a story using one of the story ideas below. Title your story and draw a picture to illustrate it. Afterward, review your story and see if you can find any interrogative sentences. If so, underline them. If not, try revising or rewriting to incorporate some.

- If you could invent a new sport, what would it be?
- If you became Prime Minister, what would you do for the country?
- If you could go to school in disguise, what would happen?

Title: _____

_____
_____
_____
_____
_____
_____
_____
_____
_____
_____

Writing a Sentence

Name _____ Date _____

> A declarative sentence expresses a complete thought, begins with a capital letter and ends with a full stop. (**I** always use the scooper when I walk the dog.)

Write a story using one of the story ideas below. Title your story and draw a picture to illustrate it. Afterward, review your story and see if you can find any declarative sentences. If so, underline them. If not, try revising or rewriting to incorporate some.

- If I could be famous in any sport...
- If I was an inanimate object (something not alive)...
- If I was on TV, I would do and feel...

Title: _____

_____
_____
_____
_____
_____
_____
_____
_____
_____
_____
_____
_____
_____

Writing a Sentence

Declarative

Interrogative

Name _____ **Date** _____

> An interrogative, or asking, sentence is a sentence that asks a question. It begins with a capital letter and ends with a question mark. (**W**here did you go**?**) Most asking sentences begin with the words: *how, why, are, is, which, where, when, have, did, could, would, should, wouldn't, couldn't, what, will, does, didn't* or *do.*

Write a story using one of the story ideas below. Title your story and draw a picture to illustrate it. Afterward, review your story and see if you can find any interrogative sentences. If so, underline them. If not, try revising or rewriting to incorporate some.

- If you could invent a new sport, what would it be?
- If you became Prime Minister, what would you do for the country?
- If you could go to school in disguise, what would happen?

Title: _____

_____
_____
_____
_____
_____
_____
_____
_____
_____
_____

Writing a Sentence

Name _____ Date _____

> An imperative sentence makes a demand or a request, or gives a command. It begins with a capital letter and ends with a full stop. (**T**urn off the television immediately. **P**lease do it now.)

Write a story using one of the story ideas below. Title your story and draw a picture to illustrate it. Afterward, review your story and see if you can find any imperative sentences. If so, underline them. If not, try revising or rewriting to incorporate some.

- If you could read people's minds, what would you do?
- If you woke up in someone else's body, what would it be like?
- If you could surprise someone with a special gift, what would it be? Who would you give it to?

Title: _____

_____
_____
_____
_____
_____
_____
_____
_____
_____
_____
_____

Writing a Sentence

Exclamatory

Name _____ **Date** _____

> Another type of sentence is an exclamatory sentence, which shows a strong feeling of surprise. It begins with a capital letter and ends with an exclamation point. (**I can't believe my mum is in the hospital! I won the contest!**)

Write a story using one of the story ideas below. Title your story and draw a picture to illustrate it. Afterward, review your story and see if you can find any exclamatory sentences. If so, underline them. If not, try revising or rewriting to incorporate some.

♦ You're at a fire drill at school.
♦ You get into a potato chip fight with your brother/sister while watching TV.
♦ Your dog runs away while you are walking him/her.

Title: _____

_____
_____
_____
_____
_____
_____
_____
_____
_____
_____
_____

Writing a Sentence

Name _____ Date _____

Write a story using one of the story ideas below. Title your story and draw a picture to illustrate it. Afterward, review your story and see if you can find a declarative, an interrogative, an imperative and an exclamatory sentence. If so, underline and label them. If not, try revising or rewriting to incorporate some of each type.

- Somebody in class wore the same outfit I did.
- I thought I couldn't make it, but I did.
- My best friend told my secret to everyone.

Title: _____

_____

_____

_____

_____

_____

_____

_____

_____

_____

_____

_____

_____

_____

_____

Writing a Sentence

Simple Subject

Name _____ **Date** _____

A sentence is divided into two parts. One part of the sentence is called the complete subject and can be made up of one or more words. A complete subject tells *who* or *what* the sentence is talking about. (**The green bush** swayed in the wind. **They** watched television together. **Our school newspaper** is printed once a month. Flying higher and higher, **the plane** soared above the clouds.)

Write a story using one of the story ideas below. Title your story and draw a picture to illustrate it. Afterward, review your story and make sure all your sentences are complete sentences. If so, underline the subject in each. If not, rewrite them.

♦ You become invisible for a day.
♦ You can see things other children can't.
♦ You become famous around the world.

Title: _____

_____
_____
_____
_____
_____
_____
_____
_____
_____
_____
_____

Writing a Sentence

Name _____ Date _____

> You just learned that a sentence is divided into two parts. One part of the sentence is the complete subject, which tells who or what the sentence is talking about. The other part of a sentence is called the predicate. The predicate tells what the subject *does, has, is* or *is like*. (The dog **barked loudly at me**. The black and white cat **chased the dog around the block**.)

Write a story using one of the story ideas below. Title your story and draw a picture to illustrate it. Afterward, review your story and see if you can find the predicate in each declarative or exclamatory sentence and underline them.

♦ You are taking a flight on a hot-air balloon.
♦ How would you change your neighbourhood?
♦ If you were principal of the school for a day, what would you do?

Title: _____

_____
_____
_____
_____
_____
_____
_____
_____
_____
_____
_____
_____

Writing a Sentence

Subject/Predicate Review

Name _____ **Date** _____

Write a story using one of the story ideas below. Title your story and draw a picture to illustrate it. Afterward, review your story and underline the subject once and the predicate twice in each sentence.

- What would you change about yourself, if you could change anything?
- What animal would you really like to be?
- Pretend you own an animal rescue agency. Write about an exciting day on the job.

Title: _____

_____

_____

_____

_____

_____

_____

_____

_____

_____

_____

_____

Writing a Sentence

Name _____ **Date** _____

> Words for people or things are called common nouns. Common nouns name a person (woman), an animal (cat), a place (school), a thing (television set) or a quality (happiness). Proper nouns begin with a capital letter and give a name to a person (Mr Dario), an animal (Davey), a place (Canberra), or a thing (Ford).

Write a story using one of the story ideas below. Title your story and draw a picture to illustrate it. Afterward, review your story and underline all the proper nouns once and the common nouns twice.

♦ If you could be anyone, who would you be?
♦ What would you do if you had magical powers for a day?
♦ If you could live under the sea, what would you do?

Title: _____

Plural Nouns

Name _____ **Date** _____

When nouns mean more than one person or thing, they are called plural nouns. Most nouns follow these rules when changing to plural nouns.

Rule 1: Many nouns simply add the letter *s*. (dog/dog**s**, lock/lock**s**, bike/bike**s**)

Rule 2: If a noun ends with the letters *s, ch, sh, x* or *ss*, add *es* to make it plural. (bu**s**/bus**es**, bo**x**/box**es**, lo**ss**/loss**es**, lun**ch**/lunch**es**)

Rule 3: If a noun ends with a consonant plus *y* change the *y* to *i* and then add *es*. (hob**by**/hobb**ies**, fl**y**/fl**ies**, stu**dy**/stud**ies**)

Rule 4: If a noun ends in a vowel plus *y*, just add *s*. (mon**ey**/monk**eys**, t**oy**/t**oys**)

Write a story using one of the story titles below. Draw a picture to illustrate it. Afterward, review your story and see if you can find any plural nouns. If so, underline them. If not, try revising or rewriting to incorporate some.

♦ The Missing Pet
♦ The Unsigned Letter
♦ The Loud Noise

Title: _____

_____

_____

_____

_____

_____

_____

_____

_____

Nouns

Name _____ Date _____

> Some nouns do not have any set rules when they mean more than one. You need to memorise these. For example:
>
> | man/men | woman/women | child/children |
> |---|---|---|
> | foot/feet | tooth/teeth | mouse/mice |
> | goose/geese | ox/oxen | crisis/crises |
>
> In some nouns, the spelling does not change if the noun means more than one. For example:
>
> | salmon/salmon | series/series | sheep/sheep |
> |---|---|---|
> | moose/moose | trout/trout | |

Write a story using one of the story titles below. Draw a picture to illustrate it. Afterward, review your story and underline the singular nouns once and the plural nouns twice. If you don't find both singular and plural nouns, try revising or rewriting to incorporate some.

♦ Lost in the Jungle
♦ Lost in the City
♦ Sometimes It Hurts

Title: _____

_____
_____
_____
_____
_____
_____
_____
_____
_____
_____

Nouns

Irregular Plural Nouns

Name _____ **Date** _____

Here are more rules for changing singular nouns to plural nouns.

Rule 1: If a noun ends in *f* or *fe*, change the *f* or *fe* to *ve* before adding *s*. (wi**fe**/wi**ves**, hal**f**/hal**ves**, shel**f**/shel**ves**, loa**f**/loa**ves**, lea**f**/lea**ves**) Some exceptions to this rule are these words: *cafe/cafes, cliff/cliffs, safe/safes, chief/chiefs, belief/beliefs.*

Rule 2: Most nouns that end in *o* add the letter *s*. (vide**o**/vide**os**, kangaro**o**/kangaro**os**, pati**o**/pati**os**) But if a noun ends with a consonant plus *o*, add *es*. (pota**to**/pota**toes**, e**cho**/e**choes**, toma**to**/toma**toes**) The exceptions to this rule are these words: *solo/solos, photo/photos, auto/autos.*

Write a story using one of the story titles below. Draw a picture to illustrate it. Afterward, review your story and see if you can find any plural nouns that follow the above rules. If so, underline them. If not, try revising or rewriting to incorporate some.

- Never Say Never
- It Could Not Happen
- Too Much to Do

Title: _____

_____
_____
_____
_____
_____
_____
_____
_____

Nouns

Name _____ **Date** _____

> A singular possessive noun tells *who* or *what* owns or has something. An apostrophe goes after the noun and before the *s* to show ownership. (The cat has a tail./The cat's tail. Edie owns a set of bright felt markers./Edie's bright felt markers.)

Write a story using one of the story titles below. Draw a picture to illustrate it. Afterward, review your story and see if you can find any singular possessive nouns. If so, underline them. If not, try revising or rewriting to incorporate some.

- It Was a Crazy Day at School
- I Could Not Believe
- My Best Friend Was Excited

Title: _____

Nouns

19

Possessive Nouns

Possessive Nouns

Name _____ **Date** _____

> A plural possessive noun means more than one and tells *who* or *what* owns or has something. Plural nouns ending in **s** form the possessive by adding an apostrophe after the **s**. (The customer**s'** receipts were piled on the desk. Many writer**s'** stories are made into movies.) When words are plural but do not end in an **s**, just add an apostrophe and the letter **s**. (child/children**'s**)

Write a story using one of the story titles below. Draw a picture to illustrate it. Afterward, review your story and see if you can find any plural possessives. If so, underline them. If not, try revising or rewriting to incorporate some.

- Everybody Was Running
- Something Happened in the School Canteen
- Everything Went Right!

Title: _____

_____

_____

_____

_____

_____

_____

_____

_____

_____

Nouns

Name _____ **Date** _____

> An abbreviation is a shortened form of a word. It begins with a capital letter and ends with a full stop. Below are a few common abbreviations.
>
> **Months**: Jan., Feb., Mar., Apr., Aug., Sept., Oct., Nov., Dec.
>
> **Days**: Sun., Mon., Tues., Wed., Thurs., Fri., Sat.
>
> **Titles**: Prof., Sen., Hon., Pres., i.e., etc., p.
>
> **Addresses**: Pl. (Place), P.O. (Post Office), Cres. (Crescent)

Write a story using one of the story titles below. Title your story and draw a picture to illustrate it. Afterward, review your story and see if you can find any abbreviations. If so, underline them. If not, try revising or rewriting to incorporate some.

♦ My Best Friend Moved
♦ It Was a Special Day
♦ The Present

Title: _____

_____

_____

_____

_____

_____

_____

_____

_____

_____

_____

Abbreviations

Verbs

Name _____ **Date** _____

> A verb is a word that expresses action, tells what the subject is doing or tells what the subject is like. Some verbs express physical movement. (The runners **jogged** up the mountain.) Sometimes verbs tell what the subject is doing by describing actions that you cannot see. (My best friend **understands** me.)

Write a story using one of the story titles below. Draw a picture to illustrate it. Afterward, review your story and see if you can find verbs that express physical movement. If so, underline them once. If you can find verbs that describe actions you cannot see, underline them twice. If you can't find both types of verbs, try revising or rewriting to incorporate some of each.

- The Missing Homework
- Vacation Time
- The Person I Most Admire

Title: _____

_____

_____
_____
_____
_____
_____
_____
_____
_____
_____
_____
_____
_____

Name _____ Date _____

Linking verbs do not express an action or tell what the subject is doing. They are called linking verbs because they join the subject of the sentence with its predicate. Linking verbs often tell what the subject is or is like. Usually, linking verbs come from the verb form *to be*. (I **am** hungry. We **were** at school early. It **is** foggy.)

Forms of to be

am	were
is	be
are	being
was	been

However, other linking verbs are more precise in their description. (The store **appears** closed. That **smells** terrible.)

Other linking verbs

seem	stand	look	appear	taste
turn	feel	smell	grow	become

Write a story using one of the story titles below. Continue your story on another piece of paper. Draw a picture to illustrate it. Afterward, review your story and see if you can find any linking verbs. If so, underline them. If not, try revising or rewriting to incorporate some from the "to be" list and some from the "other linking verbs" list.

♦ The Lights Blew Out
♦ It Raced Past Me
♦ Our Teacher Was Missing

Title: _____

_____
_____
_____
_____
_____

Verbs

Present Tense

Name _____ **Date** _____

> A verb can show when something is taking place. One type of verb expresses the present tense. The present tense tells what is happening right now. (The child **throws** the ball.) The present tense also tells what is happening now and is continuing to happen. To show continuation, use *is* or *are* before the verb. (We **are learning** how to add fractions this week.)

Write a story using one of the story titles below. Write your story in the present tense. Draw a picture to illustrate it. Afterward, review your story and see if you can find all the verbs in the present tense. If so, underline them. If you find verbs in other tenses, revise or rewrite to fix them.

- The Nervous Day
- School Closes Early
- Floating in the Sky

Title: _____

_____
_____
_____
_____
_____
_____
_____
_____
_____
_____
_____
_____

Verbs

Name _____ Date _____

> A verb can show when something is taking place. A verb in the past tense tells something that happened in the past. (The pilots **landed** the plane carefully.) Other past tense verbs involve when and how long something occurred in the past. (Everybody **was looking** at the balloons. Everybody **has looked** at the balloons. Everybody **had looked** at the balloons.)

Write a story in the past tense using one of the story titles below. Draw a picture to illustrate it. Afterward, review your story and see if all your verbs are in the past tense. If so, underline each past tense verb. If not, try revising or rewriting to fix the verbs that should be in the past tense.

- All the Zoo Animals Were Loose
- Favorite Foods
- My Hair Changed Colour and Style

Title: _____

Past Tense

Verbs

25

Future Tense

Name _____ Date _____

> A verb can show what time something is taking place. A verb in the future tense tells about something that will happen in the future. (Someday I **will do** my homework every day. I **will be** working as a teacher. By then I **will have** asked for permission.)

Write a story on any topic you like. Try to use the future tense in your story as much as possible. You may use the words in the Word Bank to help you get started. Title your story and draw a picture to illustrate it. Afterward, review your story and underline all the verbs in the future tense. If you don't find any, try revising or rewriting to incorporate some.

Word Bank

gigantic • save • handle • powerful • smile • appetite • delight • strange

Title: _____

_____
_____
_____
_____
_____
_____
_____
_____
_____
_____
_____

Verbs

Name _____ Date _____

> In the present tense, the subject and verb must agree. That means the verb must match in form with its subject. If the subject is plural, the verb must be plural, for example. Whereas adding an *s* or *es* to a noun makes it plural, adding *s* or *es* to a verb indicates it is singular. (He walk**s**. They walk.) (The man drive**s** the car. The men fix the car.) An exception to this rule is when the verb forms of *to be* are used: *I am, you are, she is, we are, they are,* etc. (Linda and Cathy **are** sisters. Linda's sister **is** Cathy.)

Write a story on any topic you like. You may use the words in the Word Bank to help you get started. Title your story and draw a picture to illustrate it. Afterward, review your story and check to see that each plural or singular subject and verb agree. If not, revise or rewrite to make them agree.

Word Bank

cancel • heavy • exciting • playful • fetch • angry • punish • humour • content

Title: _____

_____

_____

_____

_____

_____

_____

_____

_____

_____

Verbs

27

Plural Endings

Name _____ **Date** _____

> When a verb ends with *s, ss, ch, sh* or *z*, add *es* to make it plural. (tea**ch**/teach**es**, pa**ss**/pass**es**) When a verb ends with a consonant plus the letter *y*, the *y* changes to an *i* and *es* is added to make a plural. (cr**y**/cr**ies**, carr**y**/carr**ies**)

Write a story on any topic you like. You may use the words in the Word Bank to help you get started. Title your story and draw a picture to illustrate it. Afterward, review your story and see if you can find any verbs that end in *s, ss, ch, sh* or *z* that you made plural. If so, underline them. If not, try revising or rewriting to incorporate some.

Word Bank

possible • mean • find • disappear • disappoint • sweet • remember • mix • joy • match • crash • duty

Title: _____

_____

_____

_____

_____

_____

_____

_____

_____

_____

28   Verbs

Name _____ Date _____

> An auxiliary verb often joins the main verb to form a verb phrase. A verb phrase is made up of the main verb, one or more auxiliary verbs and modifiers. The main verb expresses the action or tells something about the subject. Examples of auxiliary verbs are: *can, could, have, had, may, might, must, shall, should, was, were, will, would.* (The children **had** crossed the road carefully. The football team **was** winning all its games. I **might** go to the show.)

Write a story on any topic you like. You may use the words in the Word Bank to help you get started. Title your story and draw a picture to illustrate it. Afterward, review your story and see if you can find any verb phrases. If so, underline the auxiliary verbs. If not, try revising or rewriting to incorporate some verb phrases.

Word Bank

patient • straight • private • simple • remarkable • opposite • possible • always • intelligent

Title: _____

_____
_____
_____
_____
_____
_____
_____
_____
_____
_____

Verbs

Auxiliary Verbs

Irregular Past Tense

Name _____ Date _____

Most past tense verbs add *d* or *ed*, sometimes changing the form of the core word slightly. (spell/spell**ed**, admi**t**/admi**tted**, us**e**/us**ed**, bur**y**/bur**ied**, ho**p**/ho**pped**) But some verbs are irregular in the past tense. When they have the words *have, has* or *had* in front of them, the letters *ed* are not added. You'll have to remember them. Below is a list of some.

verb	past	with *have, has* or *had*
be	was, were	been
become	became	become
bring	brought	brought
choose	chose	chosen
eat	ate	eaten
find	found	found
give	gave	given
grow	grew	grown
hide	hid	hidden
keep	kept	kept
write	wrote	written
tell	told	told
take	took	taken
speak	spoke	spoken
see	saw	seen
run	ran	run
read	read	read
mean	meant	meant
make	made	made
let	let	let
wear	wore	worn

Write a story on any topic you like on a separate piece of paper. You may use the words in the Word Bank or the list above to help you get started. Title your story and draw a picture to illustrate it. Afterward, review your story and see if you can find any irregular verbs with or without helping verbs. If so, underline them. If not, try revising or rewriting to incorporate some.

Word Bank

funny • early • upside down • prize • contest • life • huge • enough • running

Title: _____

_____

_____

Verbs

Name _____ Date _____

> Synonyms are two words that have almost the same meaning. (The food was **delicious**./The food was **tasty**. I **observed** the balloon fly away./I **watched** the balloon fly away. I can **make** the best pancakes./I **prepare** the best pancakes.)

Write a story on any topic you like. You may use the words in the Word Bank to help you get started. Title your story and draw a picture to illustrate it. Afterward, review your story and see if you can think of any synonyms to match any of your words.

If so, write the word matches, for example, "delicious/tasty", at the bottom of your page. If not, try looking up some of your words in a thesaurus to find their synonyms.

Word Bank

cat • calm • workout • angry • breeze • sleepy • turn • draw • beautiful • cold

Title: _____

_____
_____
_____
_____
_____
_____
_____
_____
_____
_____
_____

Synonyms and Antonyms

Antonyms

Name _____ **Date** _____

> Antonyms are two words that are opposite in meaning. (sit/stand, funny/sad) For example: The T-shirt was **cheap** to buy, but the shoes were **expensive**. Spaghetti can be made **with** or **without** meatballs.

Write a story on any topic you like. You may use the words in the Word Bank to help you get started. Title your story and draw a picture to illustrate it. Afterward, review your story and see if you can think of any antonyms to match any of your words.

If so, write the word matches, for example, "cheap/expensive", at the bottom of your page. If not, try looking up some of your words in a thesaurus to find their antonyms.

Word Bank

never • lead • dislike • true • last • friendly • after • hold • forest • valentine

Title: _____

_____
_____
_____
_____
_____
_____
_____
_____

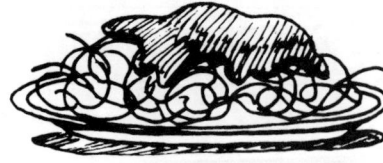

Synonyms and Antonyms

Name _____ Date _____

> A contraction is a shortened form of two words that come together as one word. (he is/he's) The mark (') in **he's** is an apostrophe. Below is a list of some words and their contractions.
>
> I am/I'm, it is/it's, they are/they're, we are/we're, I have/I've, we have/we've, he has/he's, she has/she's, you have/you've, it has/it's, I would/I'd, we would/we'd, you would/you'd, he would/he'd, she would/she'd, we will/we'll, it will/it'll, she will/she'll, I will/I'll, they will/they'll, he will/he'll, you will/you'll, is not/isn't, do not/don't, has not/hasn't, are not/aren't, was not/wasn't, were not/weren't, did not/didn't, have not/haven't, could not/couldn't

Write a story on any topic you like. You may use the words in the Word Bank or contractions from the list above to help you get started. Title your story and draw a picture to illustrate it. Try to use some contractions as you write. Afterward, review your story and see if you can find any contractions. If so, underline them. If not, try revising or rewriting to incorporate some.

Word Bank

odd • length • happen • lost • feeling • voices • book • song • white • tremble • meadow • stars

Title: _____

_____
_____
_____
_____
_____
_____
_____
_____

Contractions

Pronouns

Name _____ **Date** _____

> A pronoun takes the place of a noun or nouns in the subject of a sentence. Pronouns include the following: *I, you, he, she, it, we* and *they*. (Gail likes tennis./**She** likes tennis. Benita, Annette and Lin are friends./**They** are friends.)

Write a story on any topic you like. You may use the words in the Word Bank to help you get started. Title your story and draw a picture to illustrate it. Afterward, review your story and see if you can find any pronouns. If so, underline them. If not, revise or rewrite to incorporate some.

Word Bank

nail • right • follow • someone • trust • nature • poem • age • birthday • football • paint • smart

Title: _____

_____
_____
_____
_____
_____
_____
_____
_____
_____
_____
_____
_____

Pronouns

Name _____ Date _____

> When pronouns follow verbs in the predicate, they are called object pronouns and are used in place of a noun(s). Object pronouns include the following: *me, you, him, her, it, us* and *them*. (My mum thanked Mrs Wolff./My mum thanked **her**. I ate the chips./I ate **them**.)

Write a story on any topic you like. You may use the words in the Word Bank to help you get started. Title your story and draw a picture to illustrate it. Afterward, review your story and see if you can find any object pronouns. If so, underline them. If not, try revising or rewriting to incorporate some.

Word Bank

back • away • drop • visit • writing • talking • phone • children • explore • homework • safe • kit

Title: _____

_____
_____
_____
_____
_____
_____
_____
_____
_____

Pronouns

Pronouns

Name _____ **Date** _____

> There are two types of pronouns. One is called a subject pronoun and is used as the subject of a sentence. Subject pronouns in the singular are *I, you, she, he* and *it*. (Ms McNeil works at a museum. **She** works at the museum.) Subject pronouns in the plural are *we, you* and *they*. (Tad and Andy are great friends. **They** are great friends.)
>
> The second type of pronoun is called an object pronoun. Singular object pronouns are *me, you, him, her* and *it*. (Carol went to the party with Roy. Carol went to the party with **him**.) Plural object pronouns are *us, you* and *them*. (Lana found the lost puppies. Lana found **them**.)

Part of a first sentence of a story is given below. Write a story starting where that sentence leaves off. Title your story and draw a picture to illustrate it. Afterward, review your story and see if you can find any pronouns. If so, underline them and put an *s* above the subject pronouns and an *o* above the object pronouns. If you don't find any pronouns, try revising or rewriting to incorporate some.

Title: _____

I couldn't believe it, but I got tickets to go to _____

_____

_____

_____

_____

_____

_____

_____

_____

36

Pronouns

Name _____   Date _____

> Possessive forms of pronouns show ownership or possession. Sometimes these pronouns are confused with contractions, so be careful. (**There's** means "there is", **Theirs** means "belonging to them", **You're** means "you are", *Yours* means "belonging to you". **It's** means "it is". **Its** means "belonging to it".)
>
> Possessive pronouns sometimes come before the nouns they possess and are subjects. (**Her** report was great. **Their** party was fun.)
>
> But sometimes possessive pronouns come after the noun (the thing it owns) in a sentence and are objects. (That football is **mine**. Your pen writes better than **hers**.)

Part of a first sentence of a story is given below. Write a story starting where that sentence leaves off. Title your story and draw a picture to illustrate it. Afterward, review your story and see if you can find any possessive pronouns such as *my, mine, our, ours, your, yours, his, her, hers, its, their, theirs*. If so, underline them. If not, try revising or rewriting to incorporate some.

Title: _____

Late last night I looked under my bed and saw _____

_____

_____

_____

_____

_____

_____

_____

Pronouns

Possessive Pronouns

Adjectives

Name _____ Date _____

> An adjective is a word that describes a noun or a pronoun. Adjectives answer *what kind, which one* or *how many*. (The **hungry** child ate **six** hamburgers in **several fast-food** restaurants.) When words such as *this, these, that* and *those* tell which one, they are adjectives. (**That** hamburger tasted good. I want to wear **this** hat.)

Write a story on any topic you like. You may use the words in the Word Bank to help you get started. Title your story and draw a picture to illustrate it. Afterward, review your story and see if you can find any adjectives. If so, underline them. If not, revise or rewrite to incorporate some.

Word Bank

guard • catch • that • sick • tired • strong • decide • tell • young • active • week • weak

Title: _____

_____
_____
_____
_____
_____
_____
_____
_____
_____
_____
_____

Name _____ Date _____

> Sometimes an adjective is not placed next to the word it describes. At times the following rules apply.
>
> **Rule 1:** Except when used in questions, adjectives follow the linking verbs *be, am, is, are, was, were, been, being, smell, look, feel, taste, become, remain* and *turn*. (My kitten **is furry**. The spaghetti **tasted delicious**.)
>
> **Rule 2:** You can use more than one adjective to describe the same noun. (The **shiny, yellow, new** car drove quickly.)
>
> **Rule 3:** Special adjectives such as *a, an* and *the* are called articles. Articles answer *which one*. (Two girls rode **the** horse.)

Write a story on any topic you like. You may use the words in the Word Bank below to get you started. Title your story and draw a picture to illustrate it. Afterward, review your story and see if you can find adjectives that follow each of the three rules above.

If so, underline them. If not, try revising or rewriting to incorporate at least one example of each rule.

Word Bank

pull • ball • earn • little • important • see • real • taste • bear • world • life

Title: _____

_____

_____

_____

_____

_____

_____

_____

Adjectives

39

Adjectives

Name _____ Date _____

> Adding the ending *er* or *est* to an adjective makes it show a comparison. (The yellow chair is big. The green chair is big**ger**. The red chair is big**gest**.) A few adjectives, such as *big*, must change before adding *er* or *est*.
>
> **Rule 1:** In words ending with a consonant plus the letter *y*, change the letter *y* to *i*, then add *es*, *er* or *est*. heavy/heavier/heaviest)
>
> **Rule 2:** In one-syllable words that end with a consonant with a vowel in front of it, double the consonant before adding *er* or *est*. (hot/hotter/hottest)

Write a story on any topic you like. You may use the words in the Word Bank to help you get started. Title your story and draw a picture to illustrate it. Afterward, review your story and see if you can find any adjectives that end in *er* or *est*. If so, underline them. If not, try revising or rewriting to incorporate some.

Word Bank

asleep • energy • nose • clean • trouble • brave • argument • big • school

Title: _____

_____
_____
_____
_____
_____
_____
_____
_____
_____

Adjectives

Name _____ Date _____

> Most adjectives that are two or more syllables (sound parts) do not add *er* or *est* to show comparison. Instead, the words *more* and *most* are used. (Jennifer is the **more** intelligent of the two. She is the **most** beautiful girl in the contest.)
>
> The words *more* or *most* can never be used with words that end with *er* or *est*. (**Wrong:** The boy was the **most** strong**est**.) Other adjectives that use the words *more* or *most* in front of them are words ending in *ful, less, ous* or *able*. (He is **more** fam**ous** than she. He is the **most** wonder**ful** actor in the world.)

Write a story on any topic you like. Title your story and draw a picture to illustrate it. Afterward, review your story and see if you can find any adjectives that show comparison and follow the examples above. If so, underline them. If not, try revising or rewriting to incorporate some.

Title: _____

_____
_____
_____
_____
_____
_____
_____
_____
_____
_____
_____
_____

Adjectives

Irregular Adjectives

Name _____ **Date** _____

Irregular adjectives do not follow any rules when showing comparisons. These adjectives must be remembered when comparing two nouns and when comparing three or more nouns.

Adjective	Two Nouns	Three or More Nouns
bad	worse	worst
good	better	best
many/much	more	most
little	less	least

Write a story on any topic you like. Title your story and draw a picture to illustrate it. Afterward, review your story and see if you can find any irregular adjectives. If so, underline them. If not, try revising or rewriting to incorporate some.

Title: _____

_____

_____

_____

_____

_____

_____

_____

_____

_____

_____

_____

Adjectives

Name _____ Date _____

> Homophones are two or more words that sound alike but have different spellings and meanings. Some examples are: *hour/our, two/too/to, new/knew, hole/whole, write/right, sea/see, no/know, son/sun, pail/pale, plane/plain, scent/sent, their/there, knight/night, flower/flour, your/you're, here/hear, wood/would, who's/whose, site/sight.*

Write a story on any topic you like. Title your story and draw a picture to illustrate it by completing the squiggle. Afterward, review your story and see if you can find any words you can write homophones for. If so, write them after the end of your story. If not, try revising or rewriting to incorporate some words you can write homophones for. Use the homophones listed above to help you.

Title: _____

Homophones and Homographs

Homophones

43

Homographs

Name _____ Date _____

> Homographs have different meanings but are spelled alike. Sometimes they are even pronounced the same. (My friend **presents** her **presents** to her friend on her birthday. Why **can** we open this **can** so easily?)

Write a story on any topic you like. Title your story and draw a picture to illustrate it by completing the squiggle. Afterward, review your story and see if you can find any homographs. If so, underline them. If not, try revising or rewriting to incorporate some. Use a dictionary to help you find homographs.

Title: _____

44 Homophones and Homographs

Name _____ Date _____

> An adverb is a word that describes a verb, an adjective or another adverb. Usually an adverb comes next to the verb in the sentence, but sometimes it can be found in other places in the sentence. Adverbs answer such questions as *how, when* or *where*. (The teacher talked **quickly**. The principal **always** did her work. The doctor stood **close by**.)
>
> Adverbs that tell *how* end in the letters *ly*. (*gently, badly, loudly, slowly, safely*)
>
> Adverbs that tell *when* have many different endings. (*now, then, tomorrow, always, sometimes, again, once, yesterday, late, today*)
>
> Adverbs that tell *where* also have many different endings. (*outside, there, ahead, behind, nearby, everywhere, down, up, here, someplace, forward, backward*)

Write a story on any topic you like. Title your story and draw a picture to illustrate it by completing the squiggle. Afterward, review your story and see if you can find any adverbs. If so, underline them. If not, try revising or rewriting to incorporate some. As an added challenge, try to incorporate an adverb from each type above.

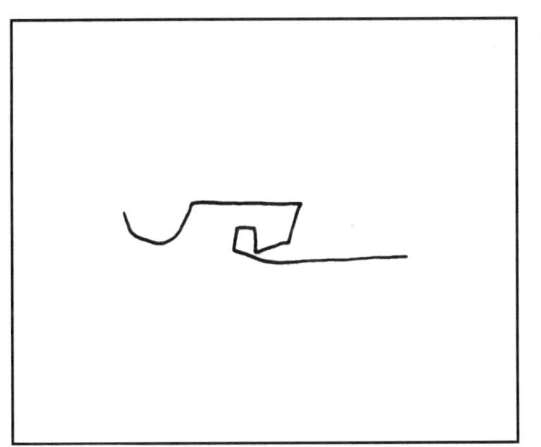

Title: _____

_____
_____
_____
_____
_____

_____
_____
_____
_____
_____

Adverbs

Adverbs

Name _____ Date _____

> Adverbs, like adjectives, can be used to compare two or more actions of people, things or groups. Two actions are compared by adding *er* to the adverb. (Ron runs **faster** than Dan.) Three or more actions are compared by adding *est* to the adverb. (Ron runs the **fastest** of all his friends.)
>
> Adverbs that end in *ly* do not add *er* or *est*. Instead add *more* or *most*. (**more** quickly/**most** quickly)

Write a story on any topic you like. Title your story and draw a picture to illustrate it by completing the squiggle. Afterward, review your story and see if you can find adverbs that compare actions. If so, underline them. If not, try revising or rewriting to incorporate some.

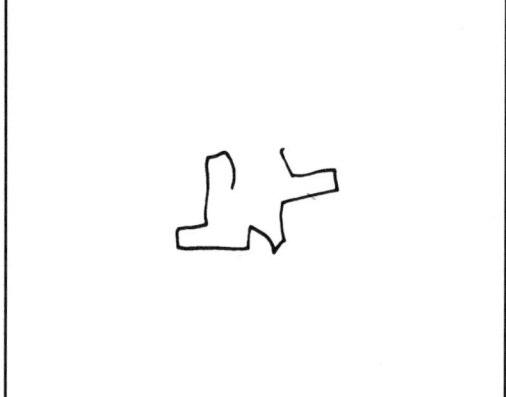

Title: _____

46

Adverbs

Name _____ Date _____

> Deciding whether to use an adverb or adjective to describe a linking verb can sometimes be tricky. To help you decide which to use, determine whether the word describes the subject (noun) or the verb. (The **girl** looked **unhappy**.) *Unhappy* describes *the girl* (the noun), so the adjective *unhappy*, should be used, not the adverb *unhappily*. In the sentence, "The girl *looked unhappily* at her mother", *unhappily* answers how she did her looking. So *unhappily*, an adverb, is used.
>
> Knowing when to use *good* or *well* and *bad* or *badly* can be tricky too. *Good* is always an adjective. (We had a **good time** at the show) *Well* can be either an adjective (**I** don't feel **well** today.), or an adverb. (I don't **see well**. She **sings well**.) *Bad* is the accepted form with a linking verb. (This cheese **tastes bad**.)

Write a story on any topic you like. Title your story and draw a picture to illustrate it by completing the squiggle. Try to incorporate the proper uses of *good, well, bad* and *badly* in your story. Afterward, review your story and see if you can find them used correctly. If so, underline them. If not, try revising or rewriting to incorporate them.

Title: _____

_____

_____

_____

_____

_____

_____

_____

_____

_____

Adverbs

Adverbs vs. Adjectives

Adverb and Adjective Review

Name _____ **Date** _____

Part of a first sentence of a story is given below. Write a story starting where that sentence leaves off. Title your story and draw a picture to illustrate it by completing the squiggle. Afterward, review your story and see if you can find at least five adjectives and five adverbs. If so, underline them. If not, try rewriting or revising your story to incorporate more.

Title: _____

I went to Sea World with my family, and it was fun until all of a sudden I saw _____

_____
_____
_____
_____
_____
_____
_____
_____
_____

48

Adverbs

Name _____ **Date** _____

Part of a first sentence of a story is given below. Write a story starting where that sentence leaves off. Title your story and draw a picture to illustrate it by completing the squiggle. Afterward, review your story and see if you can find at least five adjectives and five adverbs. If so, underline them. If not, try rewriting or revising your

Title: _____

The sun shined brightly as it rained, so I raced to school, but no one was there

Adverbs

49

Name _____ **Date** _____

Compound Words

There are three types of compound words.

1 A compound word can be two words joined together to form one word. (book + store = bookstore; sun + light = sunlight)

2 A compound word can be two words that are not joined together but still form one meaning. (light bulb, paper clip, telephone booth)

3 A compound word can be two or more words with a hyphen or hyphens (-) between the words. (sister-in-law, brother-in-law, know-how)

Part of a first sentence of a story is given below. Write a story starting where that sentence leaves off. Title your story and draw a picture to illustrate it by completing the squiggle. Afterward, review your story and see if you can find any compound words. If so, underline them. If not, try revising or rewriting to incorporate some.

Title: _____

_____

I was excited because I won _____

_____

_____

_____

_____

_____

_____

_____

_____

50   Compound Words

Name _____ Date _____

> Only one negative word can be used in a sentence. (My friend did **not** stop building airplanes.) Adverbs such as **not** and **never** are negatives that should not be used in the same sentence with words such as *no, no one, nobody, nothing, nowhere, neither*. Using *not* or *never* with these words results in a double negative. (**Wrong:** She **wasn't no** fool.) Remove the second negative word and substitute words such as *a, any, anyone, ever, anything, anywhere* and *anybody* to correct the sentence. (She **wasn't a** fool.)

Part of a first sentence of a story is given below. Write a story starting where that sentence leaves off. Try to incorporate some negative words in your story. Title your story and draw a picture to illustrate it by completing the squiggle. Afterward, review your story and see if you can find any negative words. Are they used correctly? If so, underline them. If not, try revising or rewriting to incorporate some correct usages or fix incorrect ones.

Title: _____

_____

All aboard for the trip of a lifetime

on _____

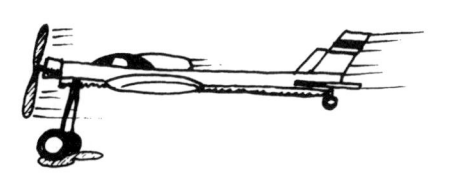

_____

_____

_____

_____

_____

_____

Double Negatives

51

Prefixes

Name _____ Date _____

A root word is also called a base word. A prefix is a word part that is placed at the beginning of the base word to change its meaning. Some prefixes and their meanings include the following:

dis-	opposite of, not	**un-**	the opposite of, not
re-	again	**im-**	not
pre-	before	**mis-**	badly, wrong
over-	above, more than	**non-**	or **dis-** opposite of
extra-	beyond, more than		

Here are some examples of these prefixes with base words and meanings: **im**polite/not polite; **mis**pronounced/not pronounced correctly; **re**read/read again.

Write a story on any topic you like. You may use the words in the Word Bank to help you get started. Title your story and draw a picture to illustrate it. Afterward, review your story and see if you can find words with prefixes. If so, underline the prefix once and the base word twice. If not, try revising or rewriting to incorporate some.

Word Bank

dislike • misspell • incorrect • overhead • unfold • incorrect • overheard • nonsense • mispronounce • impatient

Title: _____

_____

_____

_____

_____

_____

_____

_____

Name _____ Date _____

> A suffix is a word part that is added to the end of a base word to change its meaning. Some suffixes are: **-er, -ly, -or, -able, -less, -ful, -ish, -y, -ness, -ment, -ful, -able, -ible, -ous**. (My friend Mark was hope**ful** because he had studied for his test.)

Write a story on any topic you like. You may use the words in the Word Bank below to help you get started. Title your story and draw a picture to illustrate it. Afterward, review your story and see if you can find words with suffixes. If so, underline the suffix once and the base word twice. If not, try revising or rewriting to incorporate some.

Word Bank

unusually • harmful • actor • teacher • fearless • breakable • enjoyable • beautiful • hopeless • careful • quickly • bumpy

Title: _____

_____
_____
_____
_____
_____
_____
_____
_____
_____
_____
_____
_____
_____

Suffixes

Prepositions

Name _____ Date _____

A preposition is a word that shows a connection between a noun or a pronoun and some other word in a sentence. Prepositions are words that show relationships such as ownership, location and direction. Here is a list of some prepositions:

about, along, below, down, inside, off, through, up, above, around, beneath, during, into, on, to, upon, across, at, between, for, like, outside, towards, with, after, before, beyond, from, near, over, under, within, against, behind, by, in, of, past, until, without

A preposition is usually followed by a noun or pronoun (called an object). The preposition and its noun/pronoun is called a prepositional phrase. (Steve fell **off his skateboard**. Kristen went **toward the toy store** quickly.)

A first sentence and a last sentence of a story are given below. Write a story filling in the middle, using those sentences as your first and last lines. Title your story and draw a picture to illustrate it. Afterward, review your story and see if you can find any prepositional phrases. If so, underline them. If not, reread the list of prepositions above and then revise or rewrite to incorporate some.

Beginning: All the lights went off.

Ending: Thank goodness the lights came back on.

Title: _____

_____

_____

_____

_____

_____

_____

_____

Name _____ Date _____

> Conjunctions are words that join together other words, phrases, or sentences. They can combine two nouns, two verbs or two adjectives. The coordinating conjunctions are *and, but, or, nor, for* and *yet*. (I'm not sure whether my friend will succeed **or** fail at making the football team. I heard what the teacher said **and** wrote it down.)

A first sentence and a last sentence of a story are given below. Write a story filling in the middle, using those sentences as your first and last lines. Title your story and draw a picture to illustrate it. Afterward, review your story and see if you can find any conjunctions. If so, underline them. If not, reread the list of conjunctions above and then revise or rewrite to incorporate some.

Beginning: I have never done that before.

Ending: Everybody was proud of me!

Title: _____

_____
_____
_____
_____
_____
_____
_____
_____
_____
_____

Conjunctions

Name _____ **Date** _____

> Interjections are words that express a feeling and are often followed by a comma or an exclamation mark. (**Ouch**! That hurt! **Well**, he made it! **Oh**, what a wonderful present!)
>
> Words that are interjections include: *ah, oh, hurry, oops, hey, alas, well, boy, aha, oh no, yipee, ouch, wow, my, goodness.*

A first sentence and a last sentence of a story are given below. Write a story filling in the middle, using those sentences as your first and last lines. Title your story and draw a picture to illustrate it. Afterward, review your story and see if you can find any interjections. If so, underline them. If not, reread the list of interjections above and then revise or rewrite to incorporate some.

Beginning: I didn't think it was true.

Ending: Everyone clapped for me.

Title: _____

_____
_____
_____
_____
_____
_____
_____
_____
_____

Interjections

Name _____ Date _____

> A run-on sentence is two or more sentences that need to be separated by a conjunction *(and, but, or, nor, for, yet)* or punctuation, but are not. (**Run-on:** Lisa made the basket the audience cheered.) This sentence expresses two complete thoughts and can be corrected by breaking the sentence into two sentences; by connecting them with the word *and;* by connecting them with a semicolon; or by rewriting to combine the sentences.
>
> Lisa made the basket. The audience cheered.
> Lisa made the basket and the audience cheered.
> Lisa made the basket; the audience cheered.
> After Lisa made the basket, the audience cheered.

A first sentence and a last sentence of a story are given below. Write a story filling in the middle, using those sentences as your first and last lines. Continue your story on another piece of paper. Title your story and draw a picture to illustrate it. Afterward, review your story and see if you can find any run-on sentences. If so, correct them. If not, write two sentences from your story at the bottom of your paper. Choose two that contain conjunctions in the middle. Then rewrite both sentences so that they show the four ways to correct a run-on sentence, as illustrated above.

Beginning: My best friend called me last night and asked for my help.

Ending: I'm glad I could help my friend.

Title: _____

_____

_____

_____

_____

_____

Run-on Sentences

Compound Subjects

Name _____ **Date** _____

> Whereas a sentence with a simple subject has only one subject, a sentence with a compound subject contains two or more subjects. (**Simple Subject: Amy** is my friend. **Compound Subject: Amy and Eddie** are friends.)

A first sentence and a last sentence of a story are given below. Write a story filling in the middle, using those sentences as your first and last lines. Title your story and draw a picture to illustrate it. Afterward, review your story and see if you can find any compound subject sentences. If so, underline them. If not, try revising or rewriting to incorporate some.

Beginning: Everybody in the school yard started running so I . . .

Ending: Thank goodness it is over.

Title: _____

_____

_____

_____

_____

_____

_____

_____

_____

_____

_____

_____

Compound Subjects

Name _____ Date _____

> When the compound subject of a sentence has three or more simple subjects, a comma must separate them. (Dominic, Mike and Eduardo went to the movies together.)

A first sentence and a last sentence of a story are given below. Write a story filling in the middle, using those sentences as your first and last lines. Title your story and draw a picture to illustrate it. Afterward, review your story and see if you can find any sentences with three or more subjects. If so, underline them. If not, try revising or rewriting to incorporate some.

Beginning: I woke up in the morning and I found myself backwards. My back was where my front should be and my front was where my back usually is, so I...

Ending: Wow! What a fun day!

Title: _____

_____
_____
_____
_____
_____
_____
_____
_____
_____
_____

Compound Subjects

Compound Predicates

Name _____ **Date** _____

> A compound predicate includes the verb(s) and all the other words related to it. In the following predicate, two verbs are joined together by the word *and*. (Ken and Laura **listened and learned**.)

A first sentence and a last sentence of a story are given below. Write a story filling in the middle, using those sentences as your first and last lines. Title your story and draw a picture to illustrate it. Afterward, review your story and see if you can find at least one complete predicate with two verbs joined together by *and*. If so, underline it. If not, try revising or rewriting to incorporate at least one.

Beginning: One day I woke up in my (mum's/dad's) body so I...

Ending: Nobody would believe what happened to me.

Title: _____

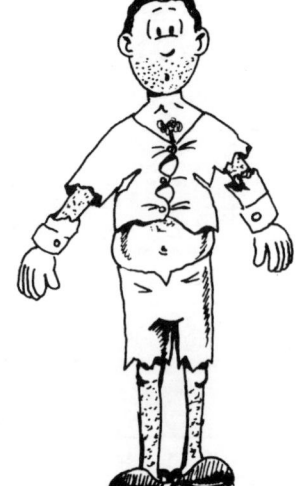

_____
_____
_____
_____
_____
_____
_____
_____
_____
_____
_____
_____

Compound Predicates

Name _____ **Date** _____

> Sometimes compound predicates can have three or more verbs separated by commas and a conjunction, such as *and*, before the last verb. (The audience **cheered, screamed and booed**.) Sometimes in the compound predicate there are other words besides the verbs and a conjunction. (Shawn **grabbed her felt pen, thought and wrote**.)

A first sentence and a last sentence of a story are given below. Write a story filling in the middle, using those sentences as your first and last lines. Title your story and draw a picture to illustrate it. Afterward, review your story and see if you can find a compound predicate with three or more verbs in it. If so, underline it. If not, try revising or rewriting to incorporate one.

Beginning: One day I met the Prime Minister of Australia so I...

Ending: I'm glad I had the chance to share my thoughts with him.

Title: _____

_____
_____
_____
_____
_____
_____
_____
_____
_____
_____
_____

Compound Predicates

Compound Predicates

Name _____ Date _____

A first sentence and a last sentence of a story are given below. Write a story filling in the middle, using those sentences as your first and last lines. Title your story and draw a picture to illustrate it. Afterward, review your story and see if you can find compound predicates. Revise or rewrite until you have incorporated each of the following:

1 A compound predicate with two or more verbs joined by the word *and*. (Sally surfed and swam.)

2 A compound predicate with three or more verbs and the word *and*. (Jesse ran, hurdled and jumped his way to victory.)

3 A compound predicate that includes more than verbs and the word *and*. (Marta read the book, took the test and received an A).

Beginning: I found a flying machine and was surprised to. . .

Ending: Wow! That was an experience.

Title: _____

_____
_____
_____
_____
_____
_____
_____
_____
_____
_____

Compound Predicates

Name _____ Date _____

> In a sentence, a comma serves as a pause and also separates items in a series. The comma also has other uses.
>
> **1** When a sentence begins with words such as *yes, well, first, next, no, however, though, of course,* etc., a comma follows these words. (**No**, I can't go. **First**, let's go to the park.)
>
> **2** Commas are used in dates, between the day and the month. (**Tuesday**, 1 October 1997)
>
> **3** Commas are used to set off a name. (**Craig**, come here. Come here, **Craig**.)
>
> **4** Commas are used between the last and first name. (Do**e**, Shelly; Smit**h**, Johnny)
>
> **5** A comma can be used in a compound sentence. (I like hamburger**s**, but hot dogs are my favorite.)

A first sentence and a last sentence of a story are given below. Write a story filling in the middle, using those sentences as your first and last lines. Title your story and draw a picture to illustrate it. Afterward, review your story and see if you can find any uses of commas such as those listed above. If so, underline them. If not, try revising or rewriting to incorporate at least one of each usage above.

Beginning: It couldn't have happened on a better day...

Ending: Everyone was happy, especially me.

Title: _____

_____
_____
_____
_____
_____
_____

Commas

Onomatopoeia

Name _____ Date _____

> Onomatopoeia is the use of words that imitate sounds. Some words that suggest sounds are: *crash, ding, dong, fizz, zoom, squeak, screech, creak*. (I heard the **zoom** of the **screeching** motorcycle **whizzing** by me.)

Write a story on any topic you like. You may use the words in the Word Bank to help you get started. Title your story and draw a picture to illustrate it. Afterward, review your story and see if you can find any onomatopoeic words. If so, underline them. If not, try revising or rewriting to incorporate some.

Word Bank

strong • empty • pretend • pleasure • interesting • climb • chase • order • heavy • found • backwards

Title: _____

_____
_____
_____
_____
_____
_____
_____
_____
_____
_____
_____
_____

Name _____ Date _____

> Similes help make your writing more alive and exciting. Similes are a figurative form of speech that show comparison by using the words *like* or *as*. She **runs like honey** around the track. Her skin **felt like silk**. He is **as strong as a horse**. She **ran like the wind**. Today it was **as hot as an oven**. The clouds **looked as white as marshmallows**.)

Write a story on any topic you like. You may use the words in the Word Bank to help you get started. Title your story and draw a picture to illustrate it. Afterward, review your story and see if you can find any similes. If so, underline them. If not, try revising or rewriting to incorporate some.

Word Bank

basketball • snail • eagle • truck • freeway • tall • park • school • football • book

Title: _____

_____
_____
_____
_____
_____
_____
_____
_____
_____
_____
_____
_____

Similes

65

Metaphors

Name _____ **Date** _____

Metaphors help make your writing more descriptive. They are a figurative form of speech and compare two different things **without** using the words *like* or *as*. (Today the wind **is a dingo's howl**. The thunder **was an angry mother's yell**.)

Write a story on any topic you like. You may use the words in the Word Bank to help you get started. Title your story and draw a picture to illustrate it. Afterward, review your story and see if you can find any metaphors. If so, underline them. If not, try revising or rewriting to incorporate some.

Word Bank

monster • flew • playful • race • finish • intelligent • heat • friendly • escape

Title: _____

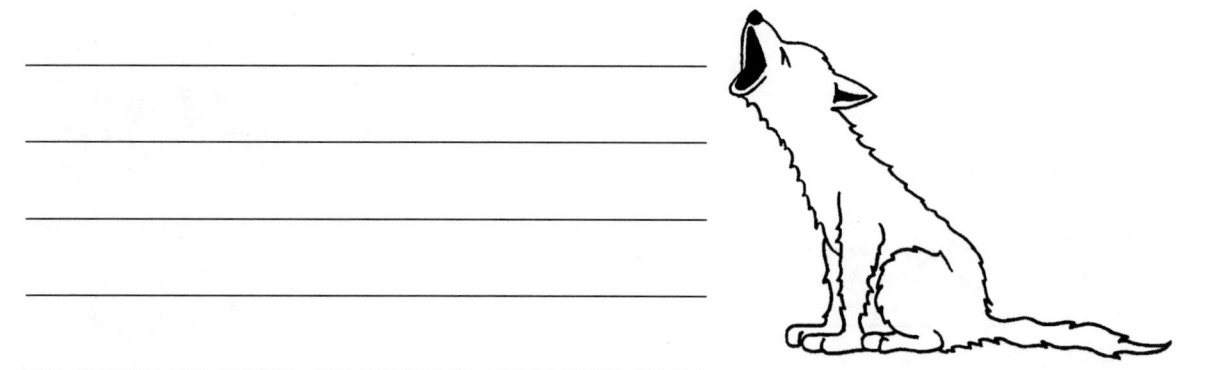

_____

_____

_____

_____

_____

_____

_____

_____

_____

_____

_____

Name _____ Date _____

> Personification is a figure of speech in which inanimate objects are given living qualities. (It was nice to feel my soft **Doona hug me** during the cold night. The **trees stretched their arms** to welcome the rain. My mother's chocolate **cake begged me** to take a bite.)

Write a story on any topic you like. You may use the words in the Word Bank to help you get started. Title your story and draw a picture to illustrate it. Afterward, review your story and see if you can find any examples of personification. If so, underline them. If not, try revising or rewriting to incorporate some.

Word Bank

shoe • tree • lolly • wild • trick • prize • stamp • loud • important

Title: _____

_____
_____
_____
_____
_____
_____
_____
_____
_____
_____
_____
_____
_____
_____

Personification

Alliteration

Name _____ Date _____

> Alliteration is the repetition of the same sound at the beginning of several words. This device is used most often in poetry. Alliteration can be fun when used in a sentence to make tongue twisters, especially when you try to say the words quickly. Say the examples below quickly.
>
> *She sells sea shells at the sea shore.*
> *Where are the sea shells that she sells at the sea shore?*
>
> *If Peter Piper picked a peck of pickled peppers, where is the peck of pickled peppers that Peter Piper picked?*
>
> *Rubber baby buggy bumpers.*

Write ten alliterations (tongue twisters) of your own and practise them with your friends. As an added challenge, take one of your alliterations and use it as the first line of a poem you write. Make your poem at least four lines in length.

_____
_____
_____
_____
_____
_____
_____
_____
_____
_____

Alliteration

Name _____ Date _____

> Alliteration is the repetition of the same sound at the beginning of several words. This devise is used most often in poetry. It is fun to try to begin all or many of the main words in a sentence with the same consonant. (**C**autious **C**aroline **c**arefully **c**ounted **c**olourful **c**rayons. **B**right **b**ut **b**ashful **b**oys **b**eam with **b**liss while **b**ouncing **b**alls.)

Write eight alliterative sentences of your own. Choose one of these sentences to be the title of a story. Then write the story and draw a picture to illustrate it. You may use words from the Word Bank, if you wish. Your story does not have to be all in alliteration.

Word Bank

television • computer • VCR • skateboard • in-line skates • video games • bicycle • pogo stick

Title: _____

_____
_____
_____
_____
_____
_____
_____
_____
_____
_____
_____

Alliteration

69

Review

Name _____ **Date** _____

Write a story on any topic you like. You may use the phrases in the Word Bank to help you get started. Title your story and draw a picture to illustrate it. Afterward, review your story and see if you can find examples of simile, metaphor, personification, onomatopoeia and alliteration. If so, underline them. If not, try revising or rewriting to incorporate some.

Word Bank

teacher's pet • TV star • DJ • free shopping • living on your own island • when I grow up

Title: _____

_____
_____
_____
_____
_____
_____
_____
_____
_____
_____
_____
_____
_____
_____

Review of Skills from pp. 62–67

Name _____ Date _____

> A paragraph is a group of sentences that tell about one main idea. The paragraph usually begins with a topic sentence that describes what the paragraph is about. The rest of the sentences (or details) in the paragraph support what the topic sentence states. The topic sentence must be interesting or exciting, otherwise readers may not want to read your story. (**Boring:** Tomorrow will be a good day at school. **Interesting:** Wow! I can't wait for the exciting day at school tomorrow.)

Write five interesting or exciting topic sentences.

1 _____

2 _____

3 _____

4 _____

5 _____

Paragraphs

Paragraphs

Name _____ Date _____

> A paragraph is a group of sentences that tell about one main idea. The paragraph usually begins with a topic sentence that describes what the paragraph is about. The topic sentence in each paragraph is indented, meaning the first word begins further in than the rest of the lines.

Write a paragraph based on one of the proverbs below. (A proverb is a short, meaningful, popular saying.) Indent your first sentence and remember to make it exciting and interesting.

1 He that begins many things finishes but few.

2 Judge not according to the appearance.

3 Better to be alone than in bad company.

4 Nothing is useless to a person of sense.

_____
_____
_____
_____
_____
_____
_____
_____
_____
_____
_____

Name _____ Date _____

> An autobiography is a story written by yourself about yourself, beginning with your earliest memories and experiences as a child until now.

Write an autobiographical story. You may choose to include your full name, when and where you were born, the names of family members who live with you, places you've lived and travelled to, schools you've attended, fun and sad experiences, friends and so on. Give your story a title.

On a separate sheet of paper, design a book cover for your autobiography. Colour it, paint it, tape a photo to it or cut pictures out of a magazine for it, if you'd like. What kind of picture would you want on the front? Be sure to include a title and your name on the cover.

Title: _____

_____

_____

_____

_____

_____

_____

_____

_____

_____

_____

_____

Writing Autobiography

Name _____ **Date** _____

> A personal narrative shares an experience in life. This type of story tells about a true event or sometimes a made-up one that happened to you, the writer. As the writer of a personal narrative, you must use the first-person words *I, me* or *my*, and share your thoughts and feelings about an experience.

Write a personal narrative. Choose one of the themes below or create your own. Be sure to write in the first person. Afterwards, title your narrative and draw a picture illustrating it.

Themes

my hobby • my favourite sport • my school • my pets • my brother or sister • my favourite thing to do

Title: _____

_____
_____
_____
_____
_____
_____
_____
_____
_____
_____
_____
_____

Writing Personal Narrative

Name _____ Date _____

> A short story is just that—a complete story that is short in length.

Write a short story of at least four paragraphs. Remember to make your topic sentences interesting and exciting and to indent the first sentence of each paragraph. You may use one of the proverbs below in your story.

1. What is bad for one is good for another.

2. Anger is never without a reason, but seldom a good one.

3. Haste makes waste.

4. No time like the present.

On a separate piece of paper, draw a picture illustrating your story.

_____
_____
_____
_____
_____
_____
_____
_____
_____
_____
_____

Writing Short Story

Short Story

Name _____ **Date** _____

> A short story is just that—a complete story that is short in length.

Write a short story of at least four paragraphs. Remember to make your topic sentences interesting and exciting and to indent the first sentence of each paragraph. You may use one of the proverbs below in your story.

1 A good heart cannot lie.

2 The eye lets in love.

3 A stitch in time saves nine.

4 Don't count your chickens before they are hatched.

_____

_____

_____

_____

_____

_____

_____

_____

_____

_____

_____

_____

Writing Short Story

Name _____ **Date** _____

> A short story is just that—a complete story that is short in length.

Write a short story of at least four paragraphs. Remember to make your topic sentences interesting and exciting and to indent the first sentence of each paragraph. You may use one of the proverbs below in your story.

1 A shut mouth catches no flies.

2 Like a fish out of water.

3 You may lead a horse to water, but you can't make it drink.

4 History repeats itself.

_____
_____
_____
_____
_____
_____
_____
_____
_____
_____
_____
_____

Writing Short Story

Biographical Sketch

Name _____ **Date** _____

> A biographical sketch is a non-fiction (real-life) story about someone else's life. Biographies can be about famous, unusual or everyday people. When writing a biographical story, you should include information about the life of the person, important events and dates in the person's life that helped shape his or her life, how this person became important or famous and how this person contributed to others in the world.
>
> Encyclopedias, newspaper articles and books are good references when writing a biography, especially when you cannot interview the person.

Now it's your turn to write a biography. Choose a special adult in your neighbourhood whom you admire and can interview. If you have trouble finding someone, choose an adult at school you would like to know more about. Make a list of interview questions and bring them and a note pad to the interview.

Here are some sample interview questions.

1 When and where were you born?

2 What kind of work do you do? Do you like your work?

3 What kind of training did you get to do this job or run this business?

4 What are your hobbies or things you like to do in your leisure time?

_____
_____
_____
_____
_____
_____
_____
_____
_____

Writing Biographical Sketch

Name _____ Date _____

> Most of us enjoy reading tall tales—stories that exaggerate or stretch the truth.

See how well you can exaggerate to complete the sentences below. The first one is done for you.

1 I was so hungry after the hike, I ate a mountain.

2 Our neighbour is so mean that _____

3 My teacher's hearing is so sharp that she hears _____

4 My friend likes lollies so much that _____

5 His teeth are so shiny that _____

6 I thought I could kick a ball far until I saw _____

7 The joke is so old that _____

8 My friend is so smart that _____

9 The hill was so steep that _____

Writing Tall Tales

79

Tall Tales

Name _____ **Date** _____

> In a tall tale a problem is solved in a funny way and many of the details are exaggerated (things are described as greater than they really are or could be). The main character is larger than life or acts like a superhuman with a certain job to do.

Now it's your turn to write a tall tale. Choose a hero or other superhuman main character and then write about his or her exaggerated experiences.

On a separate piece of paper, draw a picture illustrating your tall tale.

_____
_____
_____
_____
_____
_____
_____
_____
_____
_____
_____
_____
_____

Writing Tall Tales

Name _____ **Date** _____

> A fable is a short story that teaches a lesson, or moral, about real life. The moral usually comes at the end of the fable. Like the plot of a long story, a fable has an introduction, a problem and an outcome. Animals who talk and act like human beings are usually the main characters in fables. From the morals of fables, you can learn about the possible consequences of such human weaknesses as greed.

Now it's your turn to write a fable. Below are two morals. Choose one and write a fable to go before it. Choose your main character and then decide on the predicament that character will get into that will teach the lesson (moral).

Moral: Give a helping hand; you won't miss it.

Moral: An open mouth can sometimes get you into trouble.

On a separate piece of paper, draw a picture illustrating your fable.

_____
_____
_____
_____
_____
_____
_____
_____
_____
_____
_____
_____
_____

Writing Fables

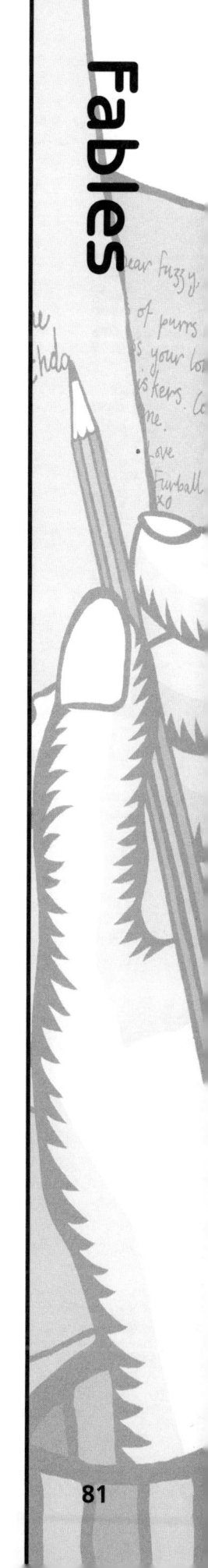

81

Character Sketches

Name _____ Date _____

> To be more descriptive in your writing, it is important to make sure your characters are real. Describing how each character looks, acts, speaks, feels, what he or she likes or dislikes, and so on, helps make your characters real.

Choose eight people you know and write a brief characterisation about each of them, three sentences or less per person. This is a good habit to get into before writing a story, and many established writers do this. Choose from your family, teachers, friends, movies, TV, sports people or others.

1 _____
_____

2 _____
_____

3 _____
_____

4 _____
_____

5 _____
_____

6 _____
_____

7 _____
_____

8 _____
_____

On another piece of paper, write a story including two or more of the people listed above.

Writing Character Sketches

Name _____ Date _____

> Characters are important to a story. You must know something about each character before including him or her in your story: name, age, gender, what the character does, what the character looks like, his or her feelings about things, what unusual things the character does, likes or dislikes and so on. It is important to make the characters appear real in your story. Remember that characters in a story can be humans or animals or even made-up creatures.

Write a story with two or more characters. Choose from one of the story styles below.

Story Styles

mystery • adventure • comedy • science fiction

On a separate piece of paper, draw a picture illustrating your story.

_____
_____
_____
_____
_____
_____
_____
_____
_____
_____
_____
_____
_____

Writing Character Sketches

Plot

Name _____ Date _____

> A plot outline is an excellent way to plan what your story will be about.

Label a piece of paper with the words **Introduction**, **Problem** and **Solution**. Read the story below and then decide what the introduction, the problem and the solution are. Write them under the appropriate labels.

_____ Juana loved animals. She decided when she grew up she'd be a vet and rescue and help animals.

_____ One day Juana found a lost dog. She looked up and down the street for its owner and even put up signs advertising for the lost dog.

_____ Several days later, Juana received a call from the owner of the dog. Wow! She felt great.

Now try it with your own story. First decide on a topic. Then construct a plot outline using the labels above. Make the outline before you write your

_____
_____
_____
_____
_____
_____
_____
_____
_____

Writing Plots

Name _____ Date _____

> When planning your story, you must decide on the setting—the time and place of the story—and the characters. The setting and characters are presented in the introduction. After this, a problem begins with one or more of the characters. In the next part of the story, the character(s) tries to solve the problem. Then the ending of the story presents the solution to the problem.

Fill in the missing parts for an example.

Characters: Anna, a _____

Sam, a _____

Setting: _____

Plot Introduction: Anna and Sam are friends until they have an argument because _____.

Problem: Sam feels he is right, but is afraid to _____.

Solution: Sam and Anna decide to meet at _____ and _____.

Outcome: Once the two talk and listen to each other _____ _____.

Now it's your turn to write a complete story with a plot using the information above. Begin your story on this page and finish it on another piece of paper. Draw a picture to illustrate your story.

_____
_____
_____
_____
_____
_____
_____
_____

Writing Plots

Book Report

Name _____ **Date** _____

> A book report is also a form of writing.

Write a report about a book you have read. Label the top of the report with the title of the book, its author and a description of the main characters and setting of the book. In your report, explain the book's plot and why you liked or disliked the book. Tell whether you would recommend this book to others. When you are finished, share your book report with the class.

_____
_____
_____
_____
_____
_____
_____
_____
_____
_____
_____
_____
_____

Writing Reports

Name _____ Date _____

A research report is another form of writing. There are six main parts to writing a research report.

1 Select a subject.

2 Decide what you want to focus on within that subject.

3 Use the library, Internet and so on, to do your research. Take notes on the research.

4 Write an outline to frame your report.

5 Write the introduction, body and conclusion.

6 Proofread your work.

Select a subject to write a short research paper about, possibly on a topic you are studying in another subject. Research it and write an outline to frame your report. Below is a sample outline. Afterward, try writing a short report based on your outline.

Topic: Cats Make Good Pets and Are Easy to Take Care Of

I Cats are friendly.
- A They don't attack.
- B They sit on your lap.
- C They don't bark.

II Cats are clean.
- A Their barbed tongue.
- B Brushing.
- C Bathing.

III Cats are litter-box trained.
- A How to train.
- B How to clean their litter-box properly.

IV Cats communicate.
- A How to get your cat to talk to you.
- B What your cat's sounds mean.

Writing Reports

Name _____ **Date** _____

> To write instructions on how to do or make something, begin with a topic sentence telling what you are going to teach. (**Topic:** How to make a peanut butter sandwich) Then, state what materials are needed. (**Materials:** bread, peanut butter, plate, knife) Finally, list step by step what must be done to accomplish the goal. These steps must be written in correct order. For example:
>
> Steps:
>
> 1 Use a knife to spread peanut butter on one side of one slice of bread.
>
> 2 Put the two slices of bread together.
>
> 3 Slice in half and serve on a plate.

Now it's your turn to write instructions on anything you want, following the rules above.

Topic: _____

Materials: _____

_____

Steps: _____

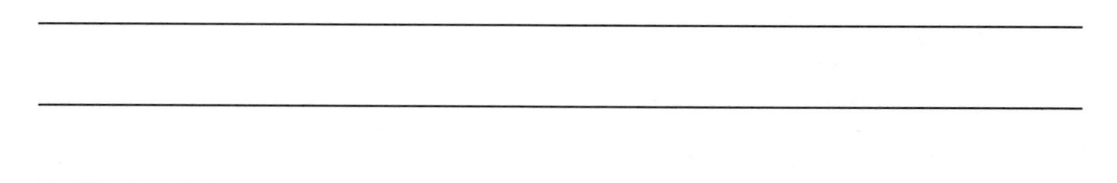

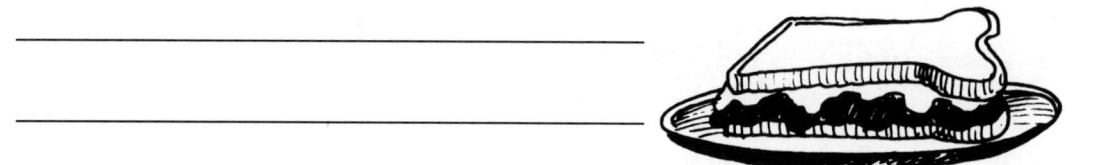

_____

_____

_____

_____

_____

_____

_____

88

Writing Instructions

Name _____ **Date** _____

Letters are another form of writing. There are different types of letters. A friendly letter is written to a friend or relative and uses everyday, informal language.

Friendly Letter:

Dear Fuzzy,

Lots of purrs and meows for you. I miss your long wagging tail in my whiskers. Come soon and visit me.

Love,

Furball

Here is how to address an envelope from Furball to Fuzzy.

Envelope:

STAMP

Fuzzy Wagger
12 Leash Collar Lane
Melbourne Vic 3031

Write a friendly letter to a friend or relative or pretend you're an animal writing to another animal. Then address an envelope to go with the letter.

Writing Different Kinds of Letters

Friendly Letter

Business Letter

Name _____ **Date** _____

A business letter is more formal than a friendly letter. Usually a business letter is written to a company, professional or official.

Business Letter:

18 February 1999

TV Programmer
XYZ Station
364 Television St
Sydney NSW 2000

Dear Sir or Madam,

I'm writing to complain about the cancellation of "The Tooby Show". It made me laugh and I identified with many of the characters on the show. Please consider putting the show back on television. Please write me and let me know what you decide.

Sincerely,

Mr T. V. Set
1122 Main Street
Brisbane QLD 4000

Now it's your turn to write a business letter. Choose a company, professional or official to write to. Remember to use the proper business letter form, as shown above.

_____
_____
_____

Writing Different Kinds of Letters

Name _____ Date _____

Another important type of letter is a thank-you note.

Thank-You Note:

3 July 2000

1111 Gorham St
Carlton Vic 3054

Dear Bert and Louie,

Thank you very much for the stuffed kitten for my birthday. I love it so much.

Love,

Joanne

Write your own thank-you note using the correct forms as illustrated above.

Writing Different Kinds of Letters

Invitation

Name _____ **Date** _____

Another type of letter is an invitation. It invites someone to an event.

Invitation:

You're invited to a birthday party.

For: Mickey
At: 123 Westwood Rd
Date and Time: 26 January
RSVP: Simone 9781 2222

Write your own birthday invitation using the correct form as illustrated above.

Name _____ Date _____

> Throughout your lifetime you'll need to fill out forms or applications for things such as a library card, magazine subscription, driver's licence and credit card. Here are some hints for filling out forms:
>
> **1** Always tell the truth.
>
> **2** Be neat and careful. Take your time and don't rush.
>
> **3** Don't skip around because you might leave out an answer.
>
> **4** When you are finished, reread your form to make sure what you wrote is what you want to say.

Pretend you are adopting a pet. Fill out the pet adoption form below.

SYDNEY PET ADOPTION FORM

name _____
        first name   middle name   last name

address _____ street _____

city _____

state _____ post code _____

phone ( ) _____

D.O.B. _____ age _____

type of animal you're adopting _____

description of animal _____

current name of animal _____

name you are giving animal (if different) _____

why you want to adopt this animal _____

On another piece of paper make up your own form for registering a bicycle.

Filling Out Forms

93

Dialogue

Name _____ Date _____

When writing dialogue, correct punctuation must be used.

Rule 1: Quotation marks are placed around what is being said. After the second quotation mark, add a comma when the quote is followed by who said it. ("I'll get it", said Billy.) However, if the speaker identification comes first, then the comma occurs before the first quotation mark. (Billy said, "I'll get it".)

Rule 2: If the quotation ends in a question mark or exclamation mark, substitute that mark for the comma. ("I'll get it!" said Billy. "Should I get it?" asked Billy.)

Rule 3: Sometimes a sentence is separated into two quotations and the speaker is identified in between. Use a comma before the second quote and before and after the speaker identification. Start the second part of the sentence with a lowercase letter. ("I wonder," asked Don, "if I can come over tonight?")

Rule 4: Two complete sentences can be divided into two quotations by putting the speaker identification in between. ("Today is not a great day!" shouted Brett. "Tomorrow will be better.") Here it is understood that Brett spoke the second line too.

Write a conversation between you and a parent, asking him or her for permission to do something. Incorporate the four quotation rules in your conversation. Continue on another piece of paper. When you are finished writing, put a number in the margin next to each quotation to show which rule that sentence follows.

_____
_____
_____
_____
_____
_____

Writing Dialogue

Name _____ Date _____

Get ready to write a play (a short story with conversations) alone or with a friend. In your play there must be two or more characters. You can be one of the characters, if you wish.

Through the conversation in a play, you tell about the characters, the setting (time and place of story) and, most importantly, the plot. Give your play a title, list the cast of characters and describe the setting before beginning your play. In a story, you use quotation marks for spoken parts. However, in a play, there are no quotation marks. Instead, each line is preceded by the character's name. Additionally, stage directions and actor directions are written in italics and put in parentheses. Here's an example of what a play looks like:

Title: Fred's Problem

Characters: Fred, a twelve-year-old boy
Marty, an eleven-year-old boy

The story begins in the Wood Oaks Secondary College gymnasium during P.E. class. The characters are sitting on the bench during a basketball game.

Marty: Fred, let's go play video arcade games after school. *(Pauses.)* Hey, why do you look so upset?

Fred *(sadly)*: I don't have any money.

Marty: No problem. I'll loan you some.

Fred: You're a great friend, Marty. But *(lowers his head)*, I still have a problem.

Marty: What's that? . . .

(and so on)

_____
_____
_____
_____

Writing a Play

95

List of More Story Starters

Below is a list of open-ended story starters. There are several ways you can use these story starters:

- As a free writing exercise. Write a story idea on the blackboard from the list below or let students choose from several ideas you list.

- To reinforce a particular skill. Provide one of the story starter ideas below but then add your own requirements, for example, "underline each verb".

Instruct the students to write a story, title it and draw a picture to illustrate it.

1. There was a box on my school desk from a secret admirer.
2. My best friend and I didn't talk for a week.
3. My wish came true when I was invited to the Olympic Games.
4. Sometimes my friends do wrong things.
5. It started raining in the classroom!
6. I made the class laugh when I. . .
7. Someone at school asked me to join. . .
8. Someone made fun of me.
9. My family went on a trip.
10. I finished all the work on time!
11. I raced down the unlit street.
12. A friend double-dared me to. . .
13. I had seven pets.
14. Someone hit me at school.
15. I got in trouble for something I didn't do.
16. I won the contest.
17. A friend asked me to lie.
18. If I could go anywhere on holiday I'd go to. . .
19. My parents are always saying. . .
20. I wish I could. . .

More Open-ended Story Starters